D1015628

The feckin' book of Irish Sayings for when you go on the batter with a shower of savages

JANEY MACK! IT'S A FECKIN' BESTSELLER

The Feckin' Collection

The
feckin' book of
Irish Sayings
for when you
go on the batter
with a shower of
savages

Colin Murphy & Donal O'Dea

THE O'BRIEN PRESS
DUBLIN

First published 2005 by The O'Brien Press Ltd,
20 Victoria Road, Dublin 6, Ireland.
Tel: +353 1 4923333; Fax: +353 1 4922777
E-mail: books@obrien.ie
Website: www.obrien.ie
Reprinted 2005.

ISBN: 0-86278-920-6

British Library Cataloguing-in-Publication Data
A catalogue reference for this book is available from the British Library.

2 3 4 5 6 7 8 9 10
05 06 07 08 09

Printing: Reálszisztéma Dabas Printing House, Hungary

Acknowledgements:
This publication has been compiled with the assistance
of a complete pack of scangers, without whose contri-
bution this book would be as useful as a lighthouse on a
bog. They are: Ronan O'Donoghue, Catherine Lennon,
Orla Doherty, Stephen McKeon, Kathryn McDonagh,
Seamus Fennessy, Grainne Murphy, Colette Tiernan.

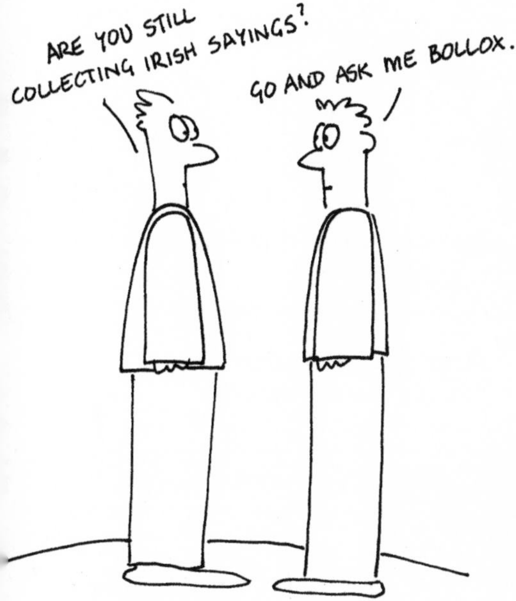
ARE YOU STILL COLLECTING IRISH SAYINGS?
GO AND ASK ME BOLLOX.

Always a day late
and a pound short.
Extremely unreliable. Prone to promise-breaking.

Are you headin'?
Are you about to depart?

Are you startin'?
Are you looking for a fight?

As rough as a bear's arse.
Extremely hungover. Unwell.

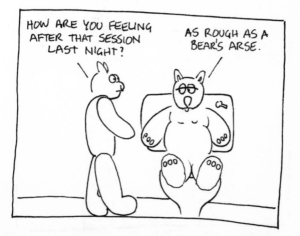

As scarce as hen's teeth.

Extremely scarce. Non-existent.

As scarce as shite from a rocking horse

In extremely short supply. Non-existent.

As sick as a small hospital.

Gravely ill. Very disappointed.

As small as a mouse's tit.

Tiny. Microscopic.

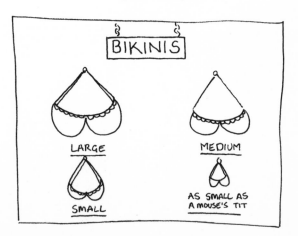

As thick as a cow's arse.

Really stupid.

As tight as a camel's arse in a sandstorm.

Very mean.

As useful as a cigarette lighter on a motorbike.
Totally useless.

As useful as a lighthouse on a bog.
Totally useless.

As useful as tits on a bull.
Totally useless.

Away in the head.
Insane. Not all there. *(Northern Ireland)*

Bite the back of my bollox.

Stop annoying me. Get lost.

Blacker than the inside of a cow with its eyes closed and its tail down.

Extremely dark (Literally or figuratively).

Boxin' the fox.
Robbing an orchard.

Breaking one's shite laughing.
Guffawing uncontrollably.

Bullin' about.
Moaning.

Circling over Shannon.
Drunk. (Derived from the visit of Boris Yeltsin.)

Cmereawantcha.
I would like to impart some news/ information/ gossip to you. *(Cork)*

Come home with one arm as long as the other.
Be unsuccessful in an enterprise.

Did you get your gee?

Did you have sex?

Eat the head off.

Rebuke in an aggressive tone.

Effin' and blindin'.
Swearing profusely.

Erection section.
The slow set at a country dance.

Fine bit of stuff.
Very attractive girl.

Get off with.
Be successful in a romantic encounter.

Gerrupdeyard!
Get lost.

Going ninety to the dozen.
Going very fast.

Go on the batter.
Go out for an evening of excessive drinking.

Go way outta that!
That's unbelievable.

Have a gander at that!
Look at that!

Have a great lip for the stout.
Indulges in alcohol. *(Cork)*

Have great time for.
To like a lot (esp. a person).

Haven't got a baldy.
Have no chance.

He didn't have a bar in the grate.

He was toothless.

He'd get up on a cracked plate.

He's desperate for sex.

He'd lick drink off a scabby leg.

Very fond of alcoholic beverages.

He'd light a smoke
in his pocket.

He's extremely mean.

He'd put the heart
crossways in you.
He'd make you extremely fearful.

He'd steal the sugar
out of your tea.
He's extremely mean.

He's a few brassers short
of a whorehouse.
Crazy. Not fully sane.

He's as thick as pig shite.
He's excessively stupid.

Hey, head-the-ball.
Hey you! *(Dublin)*

He was fit to be tied.
He was in a rage.

He wouldn't work
to warm himself.
He's really lazy.

Hold yer whist.
Wait a minute. Be quiet.

Horse it into ye.
Consume that alcohol/ food rapidly.

How's about ye?
How are you?/ Hello. *(Northern Ireland)*

How's it goin', head?
How are things with you? *(Dublin)*

How's it hanging, boy?
How are things with you? *(Cork)*

How's the form?
How are you feeling?

How's the talent?
Are there any attractive females/ males present?

I am in me wick.
I certainly am not!

I'd ate a baby's arse through the bars of a cot.
I'm very hungry.

I'd ate an oul wan's arse through a blackthorn bush!
I'm very hungry.

I'd ate the arse off a farmer through a tennis racquet.
I'm very hungry.

I'd ate the tyres off the truck that brought her knickers to the launderette.

I find her extremely sexy.

I'd have to be dug out of her.

I find her highly arousing.

I'd leave it rot in her.
I think she's exceedingly sexy.

I'll break your face.
I will beat you severely.

If he went to a wedding,
he'd stay for the christening.

He always overstays his welcome.

I'm as sick as a
plane to Lourdes.

I am feeling very poorly.

It was gas craic altogether.

It was great fun.

I will in me hole!

I won't!

Jesus, Mary and Joseph!
Polite swear.

Light on his loafers.
Gay.

Like a blue-arsed fly.
Hectic. Busy.

Like a constipated greyhound.
Down in the dumps. Depressed.

Like a cow looking over a whitewashed wall.

Wearing a vacant expression. Not too bright.

Lob it into me, boss.

Give me alcohol quickly.

Lookin' for a dig in the snot locker?

I am about to beat you senseless.

Lose the head.

Lose one's temper.

Me ould segotia!
My good friend!

Mind yer house!
Watch your back! Look behind you.
(Northern Ireland)

Miss by a gee hair.
Miss by a very narrow margin.

Miss by a gnat's gonad.
Miss by a very narrow margin.

My mouth is as dry
as an Arab's tackie.
I'm extremely thirsty (esp. because of hangover).
(Limerick)

Off me face.
Inebriated.

Only coddin'.
Only joking.

Pack of scangers.
A group of unsophisticated females.

Pile of shite.
Something utterly worthless.

Put the mockers on.
Put a hex on.

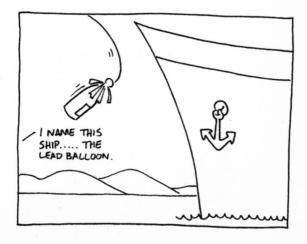

Queer bit of skirt.
A very sexy girl.

Rake of.
A lot of. Many.

Roman hands and
Russian fingers.
(Of) a man who gropes women.

Savage bit of arse.
A very attractive girl.

She'd get up on a stiff breeze.

She's easily sexually aroused.

She has a head like a lump of wet turf.

She is ugly.

She has a face like a full skip.
She is ugly.

She has a face like a pig licking piss off a nettle.
She is ugly.

She has a face like a
smacked arse.

She is ugly.

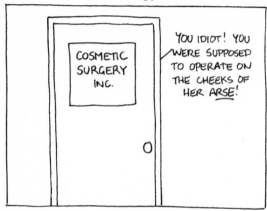

She has a face that
would turn milk.

She is ugly.

She has a pair of puppies playing in her blouse.

She is a bra-less, big-bosomed girl.

She has a tongue that would clip a hedge.

She can be very direct/ hurtful.

She's a fine half alright.
She's a very attractive girl. *(Cork)*

She's bet down with a shovel.
She's ugly. *(Galway)*

Soften his cough.
Teach him a lesson. *(Cork)*

So 'n' so.
Disreputable person.

Sound as a pound.
Very reliable.

Stall the ball there.
Wait a second.

Stop the lights!

Jaysus! Wow!

That's a fine doorful of a woman.

She's a fine strapping lass.

The mot's crossbar.
State of male arousal.

This place is a sword-fight.
There are too many males present.

Throwing shapes.
Walking with exaggerated movements,
to convey coolness.

Two sockets and no plug.
Two lesbians.

Up the pole.
Pregnant.

Up to ninety.
Really busy.

What are ye at?
What are you doing? *(Northern Ireland)*

What are you gawking at?
What are you looking at?

What's the story?
What's going on? *(Dublin)*

Wind your neck down.
Wise up! *(Northern Ireland)*

Ye buck eejit ye.

You idiot. *(Northern Ireland)*

You're only a shower of savages!

You are a group of stupid unsophisticated people.

COLIN MURPHY is the co-author of a series of successful books on aspects of Irish culture, and as someone with a head like a lump of wet turf, is well versed in the vast range of sayings used the length and breadth of the country (He is in his wick!). He works in the advertising industry, who are a right shower of savages, and there he has developed a powerful reputation as someone who would lick drink off a scabby leg. He is married to a fine bit of stuff and has two little gurriers who'd put the heart crossways in ye.

DONAL O'DEA is also the co-author of a series of successful books on Irish culture. He is regularly as sick as a plane to Lourdes, mainly because he has a great lip for the stout. He has been running around like a blue-arsed fly trying to finish this book while also working in an ad agency. He is widely known in advertising circles, mainly because when it's his round he's as tight as a camel's arse in a sandstorm. He is married to a queer bit of skirt and has three little chisellers who are always up to ninety.

HE BOOK OF FECKIN' IRISH SLANG THAT'S
HE BOOK OF DEADLY IRISH QUOTATIONS
LATHERIN' ON ABOUT THE BOOK OF IRIS
E WAS JARRED AT A HOOLEY THE FECKI
OR DACENT PEOPLE'S EYES THE BOOK O
HEN YOU WERE A LITTLE GURRIER THE
OU GO ON THE BATTER WITH A SHOWER C
HAT'S GREAT CRAIC FOR CUTE HOORS
UOTATIONS SOME SMART FECKER IN TH
OOK OF IRISH SONGS YER OUL' FELLA
OOLEY THE FECKIN' BOOK OF IRISH SEX
VES THE BOOK OF LUVELY IRISH RECIP
TTLE GURRIER THE FECKIN' BOOK OF
ATTER WITH A SHOWER OF SAVAGES THE
RAIC FOR CUTE HOORS AND BOWSIES T
MART FECKER IN THE PUB IS ALWAYS BLA
ER OUL' FELLA ALWAYS SANG WHEN HE
F IRISH SEX & LOVE THAT'S NOT FIT FOR
ISH RECIPES YER MA USETA MAKE WHE
OOK OF IRISH SAYINGS FOR WHEN YOU
GES THE BOOK OF FECKIN' IRISH SLANG
OWSIES THE BOOK OF DEADLY IRISH QU
LWAYS BLATHERIN' ON ABOUT THE BOO
ANG WHEN HE WAS JARRED AT A HOO